Words to Know

bee

beehive

flower

honey

wings

What can you find in a **flower**?

Index

eat 10
elephant(s) 4, 5, 6, 8, 9, 10, 12, 14
move 12
play 14
water 14

Written by: Alicia Rodriguez
Design by: Under the Oaks Media
Series Development: James Earley
Editor: Kim Thompson

Photos: Shutterstock: Gregory Zamell: cover; Jane Rix: p. 5; Volodymyr Burdiak: p.7; Travel Stock: p. 8; Donovan Van Staden: p. 9; Kyrvenok Anastasila: p. 11; Michelle Guillerman: p. 13; Dmytro Gilitukha: p. 15

Library of Congress PCN Data
Elephants / Alicia Rodriguez
Asian Animals
ISBN 978-1-63897-435-2(hard cover)
ISBN 978-1-63897-550-2(paperback)
ISBN 978-1-63897-665-3(EPUB)
ISBN 978-1-63897-780-3(eBook)
Library of Congress Control Number: 2022933723

Printed in the United States of America.

Seahorse Publishing Company
www.seahorsepub.com

Published in the United States
Seahorse Publishing
PO Box 771325
Coral Springs, FL 33077

All elephants like to play in water!

herd

All elephants move in **herds**.

trunk

All elephants have a long **trunk** to help them eat.

Some elephants have **tusks.**

Many elephants have big **ears**.

gray

Most elephants are big and **gray**.

elephant

This is an **elephant**.

Words to Know

ears

elephant

gray

herds

trunk

tusks

Teaching Tips for Caregivers and Teachers:

Research shows that one of the best ways for students to learn a new topic is to read about it.

Before Reading

- Read the title and predict what the book will be about.
- Read the "Words to Know" and discuss the meaning of each word.
- Read the back cover to see what the book is about.

During Reading

- When a student gets to a word that is unknown, ask them to look at the rest of the sentence to find clues to help with the meaning of the unknown word.
- Motivate students with praise and encouragement.

After Reading

- Discuss the main idea of the book.
- Ask students to give one detail that they learned in the book.

Sight Words

a	eat	long	them
all	have	many	this
an	help	most	to
and	in	move	water
are	is	play	
big	like	some